MW01006098

Praise for Albert W. A. Schmid's Books

"The Manhattan cocktail is mysterious, swanky, sexy, and sophisticated, which instantly says something about the person who drinks one. Albert Schmid's in-depth look at this elusive tipple is both entertaining and insightful. Just reading his book had me reaching for my mixing glass!"

—Tony Abou-Ganim, author of
The Modern Mixologist

"There is no culinary showboating here: all the recipes are straightforward, are easy to prepare, and involve readily available ingredients. As with most good home cooking, the emphasis is not on the painstaking or the exotic but on easy prep and easy eating."

—*The Wall Street Journal*

"Schmid offers more than fifty enticing recipes employing Kentucky's signature tipple. . . . You could even have bourbon at every meal—some hot buttered bourbon oatmeal for breakfast, maybe a bourbon burger for lunch, then finish off the day with pan-seared salmon with a chipotle honey-lime bourbon glaze . . . topped off with some bourbon ice cream."

—*Garden & Gun*

"This impressively accurate account of the history and impact of bourbon in America is chock-full of recipes to help celebrate bourbon's versatility and personality."

—Gale Gand, host of Food Network's *Sweet Dreams* and judge on *Top Chef*

The Manhattan Cocktail

The
Manhattan Cocktail

*A Modern Guide to the
Whiskey Classic*

Albert W. A. Schmid

UNIVERSITY PRESS OF KENTUCKY

Scholarly publisher for the Commonwealth, serving Bellarmine
University, Berea College, Centre College of Kentucky, Eastern Kentucky
University, The Filson Historical Society, Georgetown College, Kentucky
Historical Society, Kentucky State University, Morehead State University,
Murray State University, Northern Kentucky University, Transylvania
University, University of Kentucky, University of Louisville, and Western
Kentucky University.

Editorial and Sales Offices: The University Press of Kentucky
663 South Limestone Street, Lexington, Kentucky 40508-4008
www.kentuckypress.com

Library of Congress Cataloging-in-Publication Data

Schmid, Albert W. A.
  The Manhattan cocktail : a modern guide to the whiskey classic /
Albert W. A. Schmid.
    pages cm
  Includes bibliographical references and index.
  ISBN 978-0-8131-6589-9 (hardcover : alk. paper) —
ISBN 978-0-8131-6591-2 (pdf) — ISBN 978-0-8131-6590-5 (epub)
1. Cocktails. 2. Whiskey. I. Title.
  TX951.S41569 2015
  641.87'4 — dc23
                        2015018011

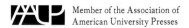

Member of the Association of
American University Presses

This book is dedicated to my siblings, who are as similar to but different from each other as a Manhattan cocktail, Dry Manhattan cocktail, and a Perfect Manhattan:

GRETCHEN E. SCHMID-JAMES
because you are a fellow Winston Churchill High School alum, classy, independent, and one of the bravest people I know

&

RACHEL K. VAN MULLEM
because you are soft-spoken, demure, and at the same time spunky and spicy

&

BENNETT N. SCHMID
because you are intelligent, eloquent, and opinionated.

In other words, each of you is "elegant and refined" and "bold and assertive"—just like the Manhattan; you are the perfect brother and sisters.

Contents

Foreword

My mom still says, "You are what you eat and drink." It is with this good advice that I give thanks to the classic cocktail movement. If we are truly what we drink, then as cocktail enthusiasts we are classic and memorable. We have been celebrated over the ages. Cocktails such as the Old Fashioned, South Side, and perhaps the most beloved, Manhattan, have made a comeback on menus around the world. Bartenders are trying to stay true to these cocktails' heritage by re-creating these classics for their guests using techniques and recipes created by the "godfather" of cocktails, Jerry Thomas, and the reigning King of Cocktails, Dale Degroff. We have always imbibed in great quantity, but recently we are paying attention to quality. My mentor, Tony Abou-Ganim, once told me the Manhattan should look and taste like Frank

Sinatra in a glass. As a mixologist and a fan of Frank, this makes perfect sense to me. The Manhattan is a classic—perfectly balanced and upon the first sip will make your taste buds sing as if Old Blue Eyes himself is giving you a private concert. Holding one in your hand gives you an instant status of high class, sophistication, and quality.

Bartenders and consumers alike appreciate the Manhattan. When its simple ingredients are assembled with the right balance, it provides a memorable drinking experience. No one is exactly certain who created this cocktail or why. I'm just happy someone did. The Manhattan was first mentioned in print on September 5, 1882. According to the *Olean (NY) Democrat:* "It is but a short time ago that a mixture of whiskey, vermouth came into vogue. . . . It went under various names—Manhattan cocktail, Turf Club Cocktail and Jockey Club Cocktail. Bartenders at first were sorely puzzled what was wanted when it was demanded. But now they are fully cognizant of its various aliases and no difficulty is encountered."

There are many different recipes for the Manhattan. The cocktail must have whiskey, vermouth, and bitters. Early recipes call for an addition of gum syrup and no garnish. In more recent years an orange or lemon twist is added upon request for a fragrant garnish in which the oils of the fruit are expressed. The most common styles of whiskey used—bourbon or rye—can also affect the taste of your Manhattan. Rye will give you a robust and full flavor while bourbon can lend a sweet, bright finish. Blended whiskey can be light and "smooth" on the palate. And let's not forget the vermouth! Red or "sweet" vermouth is the more usual variety called for in this drink. For a dry experience you will want to use white vermouth. Or you can "go for the gusto" and use a mixture of the two styles of vermouth for a Perfect Manhattan. Bitters are more readily available than ever before. The standing bartender joke used to be: "Which will last longer, your bottle of bitters or your marriage?" There was a time when bitters were used only to cure a hangover or settle an upset stomach—a bar patron's or the bartender's. Bitters now can be found in many flavors from blood orange to chipotle. You should use whatever makes your taste buds happy.

The way you call for your Manhattan is an intimate experience and a personal preference. This drink should be enjoyed the same way you desire your lover. Whether you're attracted to a strong drink or a subtle cocktail that quietly lingers, the Manhattan will adjust to be especially yours. And once you know your type of Manhattan, you will find that you rarely want it any other way.

Gone are the days of the oversized and over-sweetened cocktails. As we enter the second golden age of the cocktail, it is important that we understand what makes the Manhattan the Manhattan. This timeless cocktail is cherished among its loyal drinkers. It has such great social cachet that people of all ages consume it. This is not only your grandfather's cocktail, it is your brother's, sister's, friend's, and neighbor's.

Frank Sinatra said it best: "I think the greatest ambition in life is to pass on to others what you know." Albert Schmid takes the reader of this book on a journey to explore the heritage and taste profiles of the Manhattan. Albert's passion for the Manhattan carries you from this drink's creation to a dazzling array of what is possible in making this cocktail.

Grab yourself a Manhattan and enjoy the descriptive journey of one of the greatest cocktails in history. Cheers!

—*Bridget Albert*
  Master Mixologist
  Southern Wines and Spirits, Chicago

Preface

My first Manhattan cocktail was both a blessing and a curse. In 1999 I moved to Louisville from Maryville, Missouri, where I was the executive chef at Northwest Missouri State University (Go, Bearcats!), to accept a teaching position at Sullivan University's National Center for Hospitality Studies, fulfilling my dream of becoming a chef-instructor at one of the top culinary schools in the United States. In addition to the culinary classes, I was hired to teach the Wines, Beers, and Spirits class. I felt more than qualified to teach the wine and beer portion of the class, but I was inexperienced in the spirits section, especially when it came to mixing drinks.

One of my colleagues, Kerry Sommerville, the chair of the Hotel-Restaurant Management Department at Sullivan University, suggested that I invite a guest speaker to the class, a local bartender, Max Allen Jr. from the Seelbach Hotel. Before the Seelbach, Max had bartended at Hasenour's Restaurant, and his family tree was filled with bartenders—both his father and his grandfather had followed this noble profession. As if these qualifications were not enough, in 1997 Max won the title International Bartender of the Year in a head-to-head competition in Lausanne, Switzerland, against other bartenders from around the world. I extended the invitation to Max and he accepted. Max charmed the students, as I am sure he has charmed his customers during his long career. After the demonstration Max invited me to come down sometime to his bar at the Seelbach Hotel outside of the Oakroom.

The next week Kerry and I ventured downtown to the Seelbach. We entered the front door and walked up the curved staircase to arrive outside the Oakroom. As we sat down at our table outside Max's bar, he met us as if we were regulars: "What are you drinking tonight?"

Kerry responded, "I think Albert and I each need one of your Manhattans, Max."

"Okay, so two Manhattans. I'll be right back." A few minutes later Max returned with two cocktail glasses filled with an amber-red liquid garnished with a cherry. "Let me know if you need anything else."

My first sip of that Manhattan was a blessing. The mixture of the whiskey, vermouth, and bitters awoke my palate. It was sweet, spicy, balanced, and smooth. That Manhattan opened up a whole new world of possibilities for me—I realized then that I was passionate about beverage, perhaps even more so than about food—and beverage has been my fervent interest for the past sixteen years.

The curse, as I thought at the time, was that in embracing beverage I was moving away from my passion for food—until I realized that beverage is food. Beverage is liquid food! The bartender is to the bar what the chef is to the kitchen—plus, the bartender offers direct service to the customer and can thus get immediate feedback. So if something goes wrong, bartenders can fix the situation very quickly.

The Manhattan is a wonderful drink, the "standard-bearer" of mixed whiskey drinks alongside other classics, the Old Fashioned and the Mint Julep. Now, I often order a Manhattan when I am out, but for me, Max's Manhattan is the ideal against which I judge all other Manhattans. You never forget your first.

Enjoy the Manhattan cocktail. Cheers!

The Manhattan Cocktail

I

The Manhattan Cocktail

The Manhattan cocktail, or simply the Manhattan, is an American classic cocktail that dates back to the era after the Civil War ended. During that time period, horse racing's Triple Crown was born (the Kentucky Derby, the Preakness, and the Belmont); Ulysses S. Grant was serving his second term as president of the United States; Pope Pius IX elevated the archbishop of New York, John McCloskey, to cardinal (America's first); Yellowstone National Park, the nation's first such park, was established; Alexander Graham Bell was granted a patent for the telephone—and someone in New York invented the Manhattan cocktail. In other words, the United States was just beginning to hit its stride.

In theory, the Manhattan is a simple mixture of whiskey, vermouth, and bitters stirred with ice in a mixing glass, strained and presented in a cocktail glass, garnished with a cherry. The key to the Manhattan's popularity over the past 150 years is the inspired pairing of fortified wine with distilled spirits. Award-winning beer and spirits author Michael Jackson writes that the exact ingredients and their proportions provoke great debate. Although the classic recipe still holds sway today, in practice, the Manhattan can be almost anything as long as the drink includes a spirit and a modifying liquid.[1]

The Manhattan cocktail honors the oldest and most densely populated borough of New York City and the club that takes its name: the Manhattan Club. The Manhattan is now requested at bars all over the world and it, along with the Martini, is one of the best-selling cocktails. The Manhattan has received fulsome praise: David Wondrich calls it "the only cocktail that can slug it out toe-to-toe with the Martini"; Sir Kingsley Amis names it "an excellent drink"; Irvin S. Cobb terms it "one of America's greatest contributions to civilization"; Gary Regan believes it is "the finest cocktail on the face of the earth"; and Robert Hess characterizes it as "elegant and refined as well as bold and assertive."[2]

The Manhattan is a cousin of the Martini; early recipes for the Martini included vermouth and bitters; therefore, the Manhattan is similar to the Martini except for its main ingredient: the Manhattan has whiskey and the original Martini has gin (the vodka Martini was an adaptation from a James Bond movie . . . but that is another story). The Manhattan is one of six cocktails that are listed as "basic cocktails" in David Embury's *The Fine Art of Mixing Drinks*. Embury writes that the "average host . . . can get along very nicely with a knowledge of how to mix a half dozen good cocktails," which he lists in this order: (1) the Martini, (2) the Manhattan, (3) the Old Fashioned, (4) the Daiquiri, (5) the Side Car, and (6) the Jack Rose. In any case, the Manhattan is for people who are "secure in who they are" and who possess "a keenly honed palate."[3]

There are many accounts of how the Manhattan cocktail was invented, but three stories are most popular. According to one legend, the Manhattan cocktail was first created in 1874 by bartenders at the Manhattan Club to honor the newly elected twenty-fifth governor of New York, Samuel Jones Tilden, at the request of Lady Randolph Churchill (Jennie Jerome). David Wondrich exploded this myth, pointing out that the timing of the party for Governor Tilden coincided with the birth of Lord and Lady Churchill's first son, Winston, in England.[4]

Another theory has it that New York State Supreme Court Justice Charles Henry Truax may have had something to do with the creation of the Manhattan, or at least with researching who did invent it. However, Truax's involvement is unclear. Wondrich makes no direct reference to the judge, mentioning only that the Manhattan was perhaps created by "an anonymous genius," as Truax's daughter, Carol, wrote in a 1963 issue of *Gourmet*. In this version of the drink's genesis, a president of the Manhattan Club (unnamed) was told by his doctor to stop drinking Martinis in order to reduce his caloric intake for health reasons. The president asked the club bartender to create a new drink to replace the Martini. If this tale is true, it's ironic: a Manhattan has just as many calories as a Martini.[5]

A third story relates that a bartender in New York named Black invented the Manhattan cocktail, naming it after the island.[6]

While the history of the Manhattan cocktail may be unclear, proper methods to make this cocktail classic could not be more clear. With the recent revival of the drink in American cocktail culture, bartenders and the cocktail-conscious host can, with attention to a few details, create an incredible concoction. As those who have tasted one of these mixology creations will testify, there are few pleasures more satisfying than sipping on a well-made Manhattan cocktail.

THE GLASS

Most sources agree that classically the cocktail glass (the Martini glass) is the proper glass for the Manhattan. The glass should be chilled in advance. This can be achieved with a little forethought by either refrigerating or freezing the glass or by filling it with ice and cool water while making the cocktail; the cocktail can be strained into the cold glass and the garnish can be delivered to finish the cocktail. However, some people enjoy the Manhattan over ice in an Old Fashioned glass, which allows the cocktail to be further diluted and chilled. The customer and bartender may want to discuss how the cocktail should be finished.[7]

VERMOUTH

According to Gary Regan, author of *The Joy of Mixology,* vermouth changed the way we make cocktails. He writes that the Manhattan, which he characterizes as the father of the Martinez and the grandfather of the Martini, "as far as I can ascertain, is the first drink that calls for vermouth as a modifier." Vermouth is a fortified wine, meaning that the wine has alcohol (usually brandy) added. The practice of fortifying wine originated when wine was shipped by sea; to ensure the wine's health on the long voyage, the shipper would add brandy to increase the alcohol level and thus enhance the stability of the wine. Vermouth is the most popular fortified wine behind American bars today. The word derives from the German *wermut*, which means "wormwood." It was first made in the Piedmont region of Italy in the 1700s and is mentioned in the diary of Samuel Pepys. Vermouth, whose base usually consists of a cheap bulk wine, is infused with a proprietary blend of herbs and spices that can include, among other ingredients, nutmeg, cinnamon, angelica, bitter almond, coriander, peach, anise, ginger, rhubarb, and saffron. The differences in proprietary blends create variety in the flavor of vermouth brands available, although all are similar.[8]

In the 1880s, when vermouth was becoming popular, drinks such as the Manhattan and the Martini helped to solidify the place of fortified and spiced wines as an essential ingredient in many of what we consider today to be classic cocktails. In *Imbibe!* David Wondrich writes regarding the addition of vermouth to cocktails, "The Martini would ultimately be this new movement's standard bearer, but it was the Manhattan that was first out of the trenches." The suggestion, made by both Regan and Wondrich, that the Manhattan was created before the Martini helps to debunk the second creation story. Today, many bartenders are reviving the use of fortified wines in modern cocktails.[9]

The traditional Manhattan is made with sweet vermouth. Sweet vermouths are also known as Italian vermouths and are made from the Moscato di Canelli grapes grown in the Apulia region and on the island of Sicily. Sweet vermouth is red or amber in color, and the base wine is aged from two to three years in oak casks before it is fortified and infused with herbs and spices. The Dry Manhattan is made with dry vermouth. Dry vermouths are also known as French vermouths and are made from the Picpoul and Clairette grapes traditionally grown in the Languedoc and Roussillon regions of France. Dry vermouths have a light, golden color, and the base wine is aged for one to two years before the infusion of herbs and spices and the fortification. The Perfect Manhattan is made with both sweet and dry vermouth. The term *perfect* refers to the perfect balance between the sweet and dry vermouths. Modern vermouths, both sweet and dry, are made outside of their regions of origin using different varieties of grapes. Some vermouth-style wines are made in California.[10]

According to Louisville bartender Susie Hoyt, beverage director at El Camino and the Silver Dollar, classic vermouth should be used for a Classic Manhattan, but different domestic vermouths impart their unique flavor to variations of the cocktail. Hoyt loves Manhattans because "you can do so much with them," but she warns, "The Manhattan is a simple drink to make but difficult to perfect and easy to mess up." David Embury writes, "Interesting variations of the Manhattan may be effected very simply by the addition of a few dashes of curaçao or Chartreuse. I do not recommend the addition of absinthe." Bartender Joe Riggs says, "Vermouth is the most important part of a Manhattan." His suggestions for which vermouths to pair with different styles of whiskey to create the best-tasting Manhattans are shown in table 1. Chicago bartender and wines and spirits guru Adam Seger says, "With a Manhattan I am going for sweet luxury so I roll with Carpano and a wheated bourbon. If I want a bit more attitude, I do rye and Punt e Mes, generally two to one."[11]

TABLE I.

WHISKEY	VERMOUTH
10-year-old or older bourbon	Martini & Rossi Rosso
Wheated bourbon	Cinzano
80–100 proof rye	Noilly Prat Rouge
Tennessee whiskey	Dolin Rouge
90–100 proof bourbon 4 years or older	Cocchi Storico Vermouth di Torino
High-rye bourbon or 80–100 proof rye whiskey	Contratto Rosso
100 proof or higher rye whiskey 4–6 years of age	Carpano Antica Formula
Hot whiskey for balance or low-proof bourbon for a sweeter cocktail	Contratto Americano
12–15-year-old high-proof bourbon	Vya sweet
	Punt e Mes (Don't use this vermouth alone, only as a modifier for another vermouth.)

BITTERS

Bitters are to cocktails what herbs and spices are to food. Bitters are made from a high-proof alcohol that has been infused with the flavors of roots, barks, fruit peels, seeds, botanicals, flowers, and herbs. Bitters give "depth and complexity" to a drink, as salt and pepper do to food. Michael Jackson says that bitters are "essential" to the Manhattan, and Brad Thomas Parsons, the author of *Bitters: A Spirited History of a Classic Cure-All*, writes, "A Manhattan isn't a Manhattan without the bitters." Jackson specifically refers to Angostura bitters, but he adds that some people also like a drop of orange bitters, and he suggests that those who enjoy a sweeter drink might enjoy maraschino cherry juice. Most sources agree that a Classic Manhattan includes Angostura bitters, which Regan refers to as "the standard way to go here," but Parsons says he likes to "split the difference," using a dash each of Angostura and orange bitters. Hoyt says bitters are a good place to experiment to achieve different results with a Manhattan.[12]

THE WHISKEY (OR THE SPIRIT)

Dale DeGroff says that during the time the Manhattan was invented, New York was a city that enjoyed rye whiskey. Both DeGroff and Wondrich theorize that rye was the original (and remains the authentic) whiskey for the Manhattan. However, Anthony

Giglio and Gary Regan claim that the Manhattan should be made with bourbon whiskey. Jeremy Johnson, owner of the Meta Bar in Louisville, Kentucky, says, "You should always use bonded bourbon" to make a Manhattan. Some Manhattan recipes call for other whiskies or for different spirits altogether.[13]

RYE WHISKEY is made from not less than 51 percent rye grain and is aged in a new charred oak barrel. Rye can be labeled "straight rye" if the whiskey is aged for at least two years in barrels.

BOURBON WHISKEY is a native spirit of the United States made from at least 51 percent corn, although most bourbon is made with more than that minimum prescribed by law. Rye, wheat, and barley are also used in small and varying amounts for bourbon production. However, there is no maximum on the corn content, so bourbon can be 100 percent corn. Generally, bourbon is divided into two different classes: bourbon made with rye, and bourbon made with wheat. Therefore, you will hear people discuss "high rye bourbons" or "wheated bourbons." Bourbon is distilled twice and must come off the still at no more than 160 proof (80 percent alcohol by volume). The proof is set at 160 so that the resulting whiskey maintains the character of the corn in both aroma and flavor. Then the liquid alcohol is cut with water (the only thing that can be added to bourbon) to no more than 125 proof. The liquid is then placed in a new charred oak barrel. When the liquid hits the charred wood, it is transformed into bourbon and technically could be bottled as such. However, most bourbon is aged for at least two years.

OTHER SPIRITS. Manhattan recipes can be found that employ each of the major distilled spirits. Robert Plotkin devotes the third chapter of his book *Secrets Revealed of America's Greatest Cocktails* to the Manhattan, listing forty versions of the cocktail. While most of these versions specify bourbon or rye as the distilled spirit, there are recipes that feature brandy, rum, and tequila. David Embury agrees: "Manhattans are sometimes made with different base liquors"; he lists "the Scotch Manhattan, Rum Manhattan, Brandy Manhattan, Applejack Manhattan, etc."[14]

THE GARNISH

The Manhattan garnish changes with the cocktail's sweetness level. The Classic Manhattan is garnished with a cherry. The Dry Manhattan is garnished with

a lemon twist. The Perfect Manhattan is garnished
with an orange twist or a combination of cherry and
lemon twist. According to Riggs, "I don't think that
a cherry adds anything to the drink, but people want
them." But Seger suggests making a cherry garnish
for the Manhattan. (David Embury recommends
attaching such a garnish to a toothpick or a "fruit
spear.")[15] Here is Seger's recipe:

EASY HOMEMADE
MARASCHINO CHERRIES

*Start with fresh or frozen pitted sour cherries (black cher-
ries are fine if sour cherries are not available).*

1 pint fresh or frozen pitted cherries
1 cup Luxardo maraschino liqueur
1 cup grade B maple syrup

Fill a glass jar with the cherries. Cover with the
liqueur and the maple syrup. Seal, shake gently, label,
and refrigerate overnight. The cherries are good for
three weeks. Beyond then they will become soft and
are better used in muddled drinks such as a Caipirinha.

THE DRINK PREPARATION

The Manhattan should be prepared by stirring. Shaking the combination of ingredients produces a drink that is cloudy and foams across the top. Stirring preserves a transparent drink and allows the consumer visual as well as gastronomic pleasure. Adam Seger says that Manhattans should be stirred with plenty of ice exactly thirty-three times before being strained into a "tall, thin-lipped, chilled cocktail glass." Tony Abou-Ganim says in his book *The Modern Mixologist* that you should "stir 20 times to the left, then 20 times to the right" for the perfect dilution. Jason Kosmas and Dushan Zaric, the authors of *Speakeasy,* agree: "Add large cold ice cubes and stir for 40 revolutions." The preference for stirring is based on the size of the ice used and the dilution desired: the larger the ice, the slower the dilution; the smaller the ice, the faster the dilution. Ultimately, drinkers need to know how much dilution they want in their Manhattan. However, the bartender will be in a good position to make a suggestion based on the ice and the ingredients. Louisville bartender Jared Schubert advises that a 27 percent dilution makes a great cocktail. He also observes that for a bartender the dilution in a Manhattan is easy to eyeball.[16]

The Manhattan started as a drink of only subtle difference from many other alcoholic drinks of the time: a simple mixture of bitters, vermouth, and a spirit. Table 2, adapted from *The Old Waldorf-Astoria Bar Book* (1935), demonstrates the many similar drinks made with whiskey during this period. David Embury adds another: "The Sweet Manhattan made without bitters but with both an orange peel and a lemon peel in the mixture and shaken instead of stirred is called the *Army*." But the cocktail has outpaced its erstwhile competitors, emerging to stand the test of time.[17]

Matt Landan, the proprietor of the Haymarket Whiskey Bar, admits that he did not truly appreciate the Manhattan until about two years ago. However, he learned that "if you are going to be a good whiskey bar, you have to offer this cocktail. People don't just want a mixed drink—they want an experience." The bar offers a few versions of the cocktail: the "Lower East Side Manhattan," named for the area of New York City that Landan most enjoyed as a child, and the Haymarket Whiskey Bar Manhattan, a traditional Manhattan that gives Matt's customers "what they are expecting."

Cocktails and cocktail trends change over time. Some cocktails are popular for a very short period of time, while others endure the test of time. The original Manhattan was an equal partnership of whiskey and vermouth. The modern Manhattan is whiskey forward, with the vermouth playing a vital supporting role. While some cocktails have a mere "fifteen minutes of fame," generations of people have enjoyed the Manhattan cocktail for over 150 years because the Manhattan has a complex flavor, is easy to make, and is very sophisticated.

TABLE 2.

DRINK NAME AND PREPARATION METHOD	BITTERS	VERMOUTH	WHISKEY	OTHER INGREDIENTS
Manhattan (Stir)	Dash orange	Italian (½ measure)	Rye (½ measure)	Maraschino cherry
Manhattan #2 (Shake)	2 dashes orange	Italian (½ measure)	Irish (½ measure)	2 pinches sugar
Manhattan Junior (Shake)	None	Not specified (½ measure)	American (not specified) (½ measure)	Piece of orange peel
Manhattan Punch (Waldorf) (Shake)	Dash orange	Italian (½ measure)	Rye (½ measure)	Maraschino cherry
Beadleston (Stir)	2 dashes orange	French (½ jigger)	American (not specified) (½ jigger)	None
Brown (Shake)	2 dashes orange	French (½ measure)	American (not specified) (½ measure)	None

TABLE 2. *(continued)*

DRINK NAME AND PREPARATION METHOD	BITTERS	VERMOUTH	WHISKEY	OTHER INGREDIENTS
Chauncey (Stir)	Dash orange	Italian (¼ measure)	American (not specified) (¼ measure)	Tom gin (¼ measure) Brandy (¼ measure)
Emerald (Stir)	Dash orange	Italian (½ measure)	Irish (½ measure)	None
Express (Stir)	Dash orange	Italian (½ measure)	Scotch (½ measure)	None
Fanciulli (Shake)	Fernet Branca (¼ measure)	Italian (¼ measure)	American (not specified) (½ measure)	None
Hearn's (Shake)	Dash Manhattan	Italian (⅓ measure)	American (not specified) (⅓ measure)	Absinthe (⅓ measure)
Highland (Stir)	Dash orange	Italian (½ measure)	Scotch (½ measure)	None

Liberal (Stir)	Dash orange and 3 dashes Amer Picon	Italian (½ measure)	American (not specified) (½ measure)	None
McKinley's Delight (Stir)	None	Italian (⅓ measure)	American (not specified) (⅔ measure)	Dash absinthe 2 dashes cherry brandy
Monahan Special (Stir)	Dash Amer Picon	Italian (⅓ measure)	American (not specified) (⅔ measure)	None
Robert Burns (Stir)	Dash orange	Italian (¼ measure)	Scotch (¾ measure)	Dash absinthe
Rob Roy (Stir)	Dash Orange	Italian (½ measure)	Scotch (½ measure)	None
Rory O'More (Stir)	Dash Angostura	Italian (½ measure)	Irish (½ measure)	None
Sazerac (Shake)	Few dashes Peychaud	Italian (dash)	Bourbon or Scotch (1 jigger)	Dash absinthe
Sherman (Shake)	Dash Angostura and dash orange	Italian (⅔ jigger)	American (Not specified) (⅓ jigger)	3 dashes absinthe

TABLE 2. *(continued)*

DRINK NAME AND preparation method	BITTERS	VERMOUTH	WHISKEY	OTHER INGREDIENTS
Waldorf (Shake)	Dash Manhattan	Italian (⅓ measure)	American (not specified) (⅓ measure)	Absinthe (⅓ measure)
York (Stir)	Dash Orange	French (½ measure)	Scotch (½ measure)	None

2

Places, People, and Manhattan Cocktail Lore

The Manhattan's origins, as we have seen, remain mysterious. However, the places and people associated with the Manhattan cocktail are fascinating, evoking an intriguing picture of a bygone era.

THE GENESIS OF THE WORD *MANHATTAN*

There are several theories regarding the origin of the word *Manhattan*. One is that it comes from the Lenni Lenape tribe of Native Americans (a part of the Delaware Nation). This claim states that Henry Hudson served a dark spirit to members of the tribe on an unnamed island, which they later referred to, after they had recovered, as Manhachtanienck, or "place of inebriation." If this story is true, this island very appropriately lends its name to an intoxicating cocktail.[1]

LADY RANDOLPH CHURCHILL (JENNIE JEROME)

Lady Randolph Churchill, or Jeanette "Jennie" Jerome, was an American, the daughter of Leonard Walter Jerome and Clara Hall. Her father was well known on Wall Street because of the money he made (and the money he lost) in the stock market. The family money allowed Jennie and her sisters to spend a lot of time traveling. Jennie was the Helen of Troy of her day, known worldwide for her beauty. She met Lord Randolph Churchill in Paris, and the couple was engaged within three days, although Churchill's parents, the Duke and Duchess of Marlborough, were not happy about the match. Eight months after they married Winston Leonard Spencer-Churchill was born. It seems that Lady Randolph, as she was known, was a lady with a reputation—her nickname was Lady Randy. If the rumors are true, she may have had as many as two hundred lovers, including many nobles and a future British king. After Lord Randolph died, she married a young (very young; he was her son's contemporary) British army officer. A divorce followed shortly, as did another marriage, again to a younger man. She died after breaking her ankle trying to navigate a staircase in high-heeled shoes. When the break became infected with gangrene, her left leg was amputated above the knee; she died not long after when an artery in her leg ruptured.

LORD RANDOLPH CHURCHILL

Lord Randolph Henry Spencer-Churchill, was the fifth child and third son of His Grace, Sir John Winston Spencer-Churchill, the seventh Duke of Marlborough, and Lady Frances Anne Spencer-Churchill. (As a younger son of the duke, Lord Randolph held only a courtesy title, not one that was passed to his children.) After he graduated from Oxford, he was elected to Parliament and held several offices, including leader of the House of Commons and the chancellor of the Exchequer. Lord Randolph was the first husband of Jennie Jerome and the father of Sir Winston Leonard Spencer-Churchill, who served as prime minister of the United Kingdom from 1940 to 1945 and again from 1951 to 1955. (Sir Winston Churchill also holds honorary U.S. citizenship—the first of only seven people to hold this distinction to date.) Lord Randolph died on January 24, 1895, at the age of forty-five.

SAMUEL J. TILDEN

Samuel Tilden was the twenty-fifth governor of New York and the Democratic candidate for the 1876 presidential race in the United States. He was a "Bourbon Democrat" (see below). Tilden won the popular vote in the presidential election by over 250,000 votes, but lost the Electoral College by a single vote (184–185) to Republican Rutherford B. Hayes, who was governor of Ohio. The election was marred by disputed returns: from Florida (4 electoral votes), Louisiana (8 electoral votes), and South Carolina (7 electoral votes), the only three southern states to vote Republican (the South at the time tended to vote for the Democratic Party). Hayes's win was orchestrated by the Compromise of 1877, a behind-the-scenes agreement between Republicans and Democrats that awarded Hayes the White House in exchange for the removal of federal troops from the southern states, ending the

Reconstruction Era. In addition, the newly formed state of Colorado did not have time to organize and hold elections, so the Colorado state legislature held a simple vote in favor of Hayes, awarding him the state's three electoral votes.

BOURBON DEMOCRATS

The Bourbon Democrats were to the Democratic Party in the nineteenth century what the Tea Party is to the Republican Party in the twenty-first. Fiscally conservative, the Bourbon Democrats believed in the gold standard, that paper money or currency must be directly tied to a specific amount of gold held in reserve by the government issuing the currency. The Bourbon Democrats also believed in lower tariffs and fiscal discipline. There are several examples of Bourbon Democrats who successfully ran for office, including Samuel J. Tilden in New York and President Grover Cleveland, during a time of Republican political domination in U.S. politics. The Bourbon wing of the Democratic Party faded away at the beginning of the twentieth century.

THE WHISKEY RING

In 1875, Republican Benjamin Helm Bristow, the U.S. secretary of the treasury, broke a powerful political ring that had siphoned off millions of federal tax dollars from the production and sale of liquor. There were 110 convictions, and over $3 million in taxes were recovered, mostly from Republican politicians.

J. P. MORGAN

John Pierpont "J. P." Morgan was one of the most influential men in business and politics in the late nineteenth and early twentieth centuries. He was also very wealthy. As such, his preferences and habits were closely followed by others—and J. P. Morgan enjoyed a Manhattan every day at the close of trading on Wall Street.[2]

3

Recipes

The Manhattan cocktail has many incarnations. As mentioned earlier, classically and in theory, the Manhattan is a simple mixture of whiskey, vermouth, and bitters presented in a cocktail glass and garnished with a cherry. While this basic recipe is still popular today, in practice, the Manhattan can be almost anything as long as the drink includes a spirit and a modifying liquid agent. For this reason the first two recipes below are those of the official United States Bartenders' Guild (USBG) and the official International Bartenders' Association (IBA), respectively, both of which will serve as a baseline for the other Manhattan cocktails featured in this book.

USBG MANHATTAN

2 ounces (6 cl.) bourbon or rye whiskey
1 ounce (3 cl.) sweet vermouth
Dash Angostura bitters

Pour all ingredients over ice in a mixing glass. Stir the drink and strain into a chilled cocktail glass. Garnish with a cocktail cherry.

IBA MANHATTAN

5 cl. rye or Canadian whiskey
2 cl. sweet red vermouth
Dash of Angostura bitters

Stir over ice, strain into a chilled glass, garnish with a maraschino cherry, and serve straight up.

HISTORICAL MANHATTAN COCKTAILS

To better understand the Manhattan and this cocktail's evolution though time, we should first look to the early mentions of the Manhattan cocktail so we can chart how this drink evolved from equal parts vermouth and whiskey to a whiskey-forward drink that has vermouth playing a supporting role. In addition, we are introduced to some very interesting historical figures we don't see elsewhere in history, including bartenders such as Jerry Thomas.

JERRY THOMAS'S MANHATTAN

Jerry Thomas, known during his life and among bartenders today as "the Professor," is considered to be the "Father of American Mixology." He is the author of The Bar-tender's Guide, *originally published in 1862 and the first drink book to appear in the United States. He was a great bartender. Below is the Professor's recipe for a Manhattan, listed in the 1887 edition of his book.[1]*

2 dashes curaçao or maraschino
1 pony rye whiskey
1 wineglass vermouth
3 dashes Boker's bitters
2 small lumps ice

Shake up well and strain into a claret glass. Put a quarter slice of lemon in the glass and serve. If the customer prefers a very sweet drink, use also 2 dashes of gum syrup.

O. H. BYRON'S MANHATTAN COCKTAIL #1

The first mention of the Manhattan in print is found in O. H. Byron's Modern Bartender's Guide *in 1884.* [2]

1 pony French vermouth
½ pony whiskey
3 or 4 dashes Angostura bitters
3 dashes gum syrup

Combine in a small wineglass.

O. H. BYRON'S MANHATTAN COCKTAIL #2

2 dashes curaçao
2 dashes Angostura bitters
½ wineglass whiskey
½ wineglass Italian vermouth

Stir well over fine ice and strain into a cocktail glass.

SPEAKEASY MANHATTAN COCKTAIL

This recipe comes from the 2010 book Speakeasy, *by Jason Kosmas and Dushan Zaric. This is a close approximation of the Manhattan cocktail as it was served in the late nineteenth century. A similar cocktail can be found in* Schiller's Liquor Bar: Classic Cocktails; *author Keith McNally says this is close to Jerry Thomas's recipe.* [3]

1½ ounces Rittenhouse rye 100 proof rye whiskey
1¾ ounces Dolin Rouge sweet vermouth
½ ounce Grand Marnier
3 dashes Angostura bitters
1 lemon twist, for garnish

Pour the whiskey, vermouth, liqueur, and bitters into a mixing glass. Add large, cold ice cubes and stir for 40 revolutions. Strain into a chilled cocktail glass. Garnish with the lemon twist.

THE FOURTH REGIMENT

While this next cocktail is not technically a Manhattan, it is in the Manhattan style. This drink comes from a small book published in about 1889 titled 282 Mixed Drinks from the Private Records of a Bartender of the Olden Days. *The drink is featured by Robert Hess and separately by Jamie Boudreau, both on the Small Screen Network.*

1 ounce rye whiskey
1 ounce sweet vermouth
Dash Bitter Truth orange bitters
Dash Bitter Truth celery bitters
Dash Bitter Truth creole bitters

Stir all ingredients in a mixing glass with ice. Strain into a cocktail glass. Garnish with a lemon twist.

NYC BARTENDERS' ASSOCIATION
MANHATTAN #1

By 1895 the Manhattan was well entrenched in the New York bartending landscape. The Official Handbook and Guide *of the Bartenders' Association of New York City included two versions of the Manhattan cocktail. In both of these recipes vermouth plays a larger role than in modern versions of the Manhattan.[4]*

2 dashes gum syrup
3 dashes Caroni bitters
½ pony whiskey
1 pony vermouth

Mix well in a small wineglass.

NYC BARTENDERS' ASSOCIATION
MANHATTAN #2

2 dashes curaçao
2 dashes Caroni bitters
½ wineglass whiskey
½ wineglass Italian vermouth

Fill small bar glass with fine ice, mix well, and strain into a cocktail glass.

DALY'S MANHATTAN COCKTAIL

This Manhattan come from Daly's Bartenders' Encyclopedia, *by Tim Daly (1903). In this version the whiskey and vermouth are equal partners. Tim Daly was a bartender with over twenty years' experience when he wrote this book, which was intended for the professional or aspiring barkeep. The introduction includes advice on how to keep a clean and sanitary bar and information about the Bartenders' Union: Daly wrote that he was a "firm believer in unions."[5]*

Dash Angostura bitters
½ wineglass whiskey
½ wineglass vermouth

Half fill a mixing glass with fine ice; add remaining ingredients. Stir with a spoon, strain into a cocktail glass, put in a cherry or olive, and serve.

DALY'S BOTTLE OF MANHATTAN COCKTAIL

In addition to the individual-portion Manhattan, Daly also included in his book recipes for pre-made batches of Manhattans, Martinis, and whiskey cocktails, suggesting that these three cocktails were most popular at his bar. He saved time and effort when he had a busy bar by having these cocktails ready to go. All the bartender had to do was pour a portion from the prepared bottle into a mixing glass with ice, stir, and strain the drink into a waiting chilled cocktail glass. In the recipe, Daly writes, "Place an attractive label on the bottle, and you will have a bottle of cocktail that will please your most exacting patron."[6]

½ wineglass gum syrup
½ pony Angostura bitters
1 pony orange curaçao
⅓ bottle vermouth
⅔ bottle good whiskey

Half fill a bar shaker with fine ice and mix gum syrup, bitters, and curaçao. Add vermouth and whiskey. Stir well with a long bar spoon, strain into a full quart bottle, and cork.

IRVIN SHREWSBURY COBB'S
MANHATTAN (DRY)

Kentuckian Irvin Shrewsbury Cobb was a writer, humorist, and actor known as the Duke of Paducah. His many books include Irvin S. Cobb's Own Recipe Book, *published in 1934—the first full year after the repeal of Prohibition.[7] Cobb's recipe shows a move from equal parts vermouth and whiskey to a whiskey-forward Manhattan cocktail. Even though Cobb features sweet Italian vermouth, he calls this Manhattan "dry."*

2/3 measure Four Roses or Paul Jones whiskey
1/3 measure Italian vermouth
Dash Angostura bitters

Stir well with cracked ice, strain, and serve with cherry. "If you like your Manhattan still dryer, substitute French Vermouth for Italian, and twist of Lemon Peel instead of cherry. If recipe given is too dry for you, make the drink half and half, whiskey and Italian Vermouth."

THE OLD HOUSE MANHATTAN

The Old House Restaurant was located on South Fifth Street in downtown Louisville from 1946 to 1995. Many notable people dined there, including Tex Ritter, Walt Disney, Rocky Marciano, and former presidents Gerald Ford and Ronald Reagan. In 1969, the then owner Erma Biesel Dick wrote a cookbook, The Old House Holiday and Party Cookbook. *In the cocktail chapter she lists the twelve most popular cocktails served at the Old House, including the second most popular, the Manhattan, and the eighth most popular, the Rob Roy.*[8]

¾ ounce sweet vermouth
1½ ounces bourbon whiskey
Dash bitters

Stir well in mixing glass with a few pieces of cracked ice. Strain into cocktail glass and drop in a cherry.

THE SAVOY MANHATTAN COCKTAIL

The Savoy Hotel in London serves up a very Classic Manhattan.

Dash Angostura bitters
²/₃ measure rye whiskey
¹/₃ measure sweet vermouth

Stir well and strain into a cocktail glass. Serve with a maraschino cherry.

BACARDI MANHATTAN

The following Manhattan was found in The Bacardi Party Book *(1972). This small pamphlet contains many cocktails made with Bacardi, including seven recipes for Daiquiris and fourteen different punches as well as the Bacardi cocktail. This recipe for the Manhattan asks for dark or aged rum. The picture for the Bacardi Manhattan shows a drink served over ice.[9]*

2 or 3 parts Bacardi dark or Añejo brand rum
1 part sweet vermouth
Dash of Angostura bitters

Pour ingredients over cracked ice. Stir and strain into cocktail glass or pour over the rocks. Add cherry. For a Dry Manhattan, use 1 part dry vermouth. For a Perfect Manhattan, use ½ part dry vermouth and ½ part sweet vermouth. Garnish with a lemon or orange twist.

MAX ALLEN'S MANHATTAN

Max Allen was the 1997 International Bartender of the Year. He worked at the Seelbach Hotel in Louisville, Kentucky, and the bar outside the Oakroom is Max's Bar. Here is Max's personal recipe for the Manhattan.

Dash each Angostura and Peychaud bitters
Splash Grenadine
½ ounce sweet vermouth
2½ ounces Woodford Reserve Kentucky bourbon

Fill mixing glass with ice, add the above ingredients, and stir. Strain into a chilled cocktail glass. Garnish with a cherry.

SIR KINGSLEY AMIS'S (WHISKEY) MANHATTAN

Sir Kingsley Amis was a British novelist. He enjoyed a whiskey-forward Manhattan, as is demonstrated by his four to one ratio of whiskey to vermouth. Amis claimed that the Manhattan should be made with bourbon and is "in practice the not very energetic man's Old Fashioned, and is an excellent drink, though never, I think, as good as a properly made Old Fashioned."[10]

4 parts bourbon whiskey
1 part Italian (red) vermouth
Dash or so Angostura bitters
1 maraschino cherry

Stir the liquids together very thoroughly before adding ice cubes and fruit.

DALE DEGROFF'S MANHATTAN

Dale DeGroff (aka King Cocktail) was the 2009 winner of the James Beard Award for Outstanding Wine & Spirits Professional and five-time James Beard Award nominee. DeGroff ran the bar at the Rainbow Room in New York City for over a decade. Anthony Bourdain calls DeGroff "the Oracle, the Yoda, the walking Buddha of mixology." If you are involved in an argument about a cocktail, Bourdain maintains, "whoever quotes DeGroff wins." DeGroff is now a consultant. In both of his books, The Craft of the Cocktail *and* The Essential Cocktail, *DeGroff suggests using blended or straight whiskey in his Manhattan recipe. However, he says, the Manhattan is the "quintessential rye cocktail—except in Minnesota and Wisconsin where they prefer Brandy Manhattans." He attributes his use of blended whiskey to the practice of the era during and after Prohibition, when Canadian whiskey was used as a substitute for rye. DeGroff points out the many ways that a Manhattan can be adapted, listing no fewer than six more recipes, not counting the Rob Roy variations (see table 3).[11]*

2 ounces blended whiskey
1 ounce Italian sweet vermouth
2 dashes Angostura bitters
1 maraschino cherry, for garnish

Stir the whiskey, vermouth, and bitters in a mixing glass with ice. Strain into a chilled cocktail glass and garnish with the cherry.

ROBERT HESS'S MANHATTAN

Robert Hess, the founder of www.drinkboy.com, takes a culinary approach to his cocktail creation. He is the author of The Essential Bartender's Pocket Guide *and the host and producer of* The Cocktail Spirit *on the Small Screen Network, which can be viewed on YouTube. In this recipe, Hess breaks from the classic recipe, increasing the presence and influence of the whiskey and downplaying the vermouth.*

2½ ounces American rye or bourbon whiskey
¾ ounce sweet vermouth
Dash Angostura bitters

Stir with ice. Strain into a cocktail glass. Garnish with a cherry.

TABLE 3.

Name	Whiskey	Modifier	Bitters	Garnish
Apple Manhattan	Maker's Mark bourbon	Berentzen's apple liqueur	None	Slice of Granny Smith apple
Bull's Manhattan	Jack Daniel's whiskey	Dry vermouth and Benedictine	None	Lemon peel
Eastern Manhattan	Suntory Royal whisky	Pernod and sweet vermouth	None	Cherry
Manhattan East	Bourbon	Domaine de Canton and dry sake	Gary Regan's orange	Flamed orange peel
Millionaire's Manhattan	Woodford Reserve bourbon	Grand Marnier Centenaire, pineapple juice and orgeat	None	Gold flakes on the rim
Red Manhattan	Absolut Kurant	Saint Raphael Apértif de France	Angostura	Cherry

DAVID RENTON'S MANHATTAN

David Renton, author of David Renton's Dorchester Cocktail Book, *characterizes the Manhattan a before-dinner drink. He suggests creating drinks by "measures," or comparing the relative amounts of ingredients. In this recipe, for every ¾ of a measure of rye whiskey, the bartender should use ¼ measure of vermouth.*[12]

¾ measure rye whiskey
¼ measure sweet vermouth
2 dashes Angostura bitters

Pour the ingredients into a mixing glass over ice and stir to chill. Then pour into a cocktail glass and decorate with a cherry. Serve with or without ice. "A dry Manhattan is made with dry vermouth. A perfect Manhattan has both the sweet and dry vermouth."

ARNAUD'S MANHATTAN

Arnaud's is one of the best elite restaurants in New Orleans, assessed by reputation, menu, and length of operation. Established by Count Arnaud Cazenave in 1918, Arnaud's features Creole cuisine. Arnaud's bar, which is named for another classic cocktail, the French 75, features a bust of Sir Winston Churchill and is also known for other local cocktails: the Sazerac, Milk Punch, and Ramos Gin Fizz.[13]

1½ ounces rye whiskey
½ ounce sweet vermouth
Dash bitters
Maraschino cherries

Combine whiskey, sweet vermouth, and bitters in a cocktail shaker with a scoop of crushed ice. Shake vigorously and strain into a chilled cocktail glass. Garnish with a cherry.

THE MONKEY BAR MANHATTAN

The Monkey Bar opened in New York City in 1936. The bartenders there use Jack Daniel's Single Barrel whiskey for their Manhattan because "you're sure to get a rich, smooth, and not-so-sweet whiskey." Also, they choose to shake this cocktail.[14]

2 ounces Jack Daniel's Single Barrel whiskey
1 ounce sweet vermouth
2 dashes Angostura bitters
1 maraschino cherry

In a cocktail shaker, combine the whiskey, vermouth, and bitters. Add ice, cover, and shake thoroughly. Strain into a chilled cocktail glass. Garnish with the cherry.

THE BIRD DOG MANHATTAN

Lara Nixon is the owner of Bad Dog Bitters in Austin, Texas. She is the author of A Is for Absinthe: A Spirited Book of ABC's—*a book for the children of bartenders and for adults alike. I could not resist creating a traditional Manhattan with some of her Bad Dog Sarsaparilla Dry bitters. Enjoy![15]*

2¼ ounces Wild Turkey bourbon 81 or 101
¾ ounce Cocchi Storico Vermouth di Torino
2 dashes Bad Dog Sarsaparilla Dry bitters
2 homemade cherries (see Adam Seger's recipe in
    the first chapter)

Fill a mixing glass ¾ full with ice. Add the bourbon, vermouth, and bitters and stir the mixture until chilled (no more than 40 stirs). Strain into a frosted Martini glass, add the cherries on a fruit spear, and serve.

DERBY CITY MANHATTAN

I created this recipe to honor the city of Louisville. All of the ingredients originate in the metro area and are owned or distributed by companies there.

2½ ounces Old Forester Bourbon or
    Evan Williams bourbon
1 ounce Martini Rosso
2 dashes BD Barrel Aged Sorghum bitters
1 orange twist

Fill a mixing glass ¾ full with ice. Add the bourbon, vermouth, and bitters and stir the mixture until chilled (no more than 40 stirs). Strain into a frosted Martini glass, flame an orange twist over the glass, discard the twist, and serve.

HOW TO FLAME AN ORANGE PEEL

Cut a classic oval orange peel twist (about 1½ inches long).

Have the cocktail ready.

Light a match.

Hold the orange twist between your thumb and forefinger about 4 inches above the drink.

Squeeze the orange peel and allow the orange oil to ignite by the flame and fall into the drink.

Discard the orange peel.

METROPOLITAN

If you live in Minnesota or Wisconsin you might like your Manhattans made with brandy. A close cousin of the Manhattan is the Metropolitan, which is a little more spirit forward than the traditional Brandy Manhattan. In his book See, Mix, Drink: A Refreshingly Simple Guide to Crafting the World's Most Popular Cocktails, *Brian Murphy provides a visual layout of how to make cocktails. For the Metropolitan a picture of a cocktail glass displays color-coded lines showing how much of the different ingredients to add. He also gives a recipe for the Manhattan. He lists the calorie count of each drink: the Metropolitan has 164 calories and the Manhattan 189.*[16]

1½ ounces brandy
1 ounce sweet vermouth
1 teaspoon superfine sugar
2 dashes Angostura bitters
1 cherry

Combine brandy, sweet vermouth, superfine sugar, and Angostura bitters in a cocktail shaker. Shake with ice. Strain into a chilled cocktail glass. Garnish with a cherry.

THE DRY MANHATTAN

A Dry Manhattan is made with dry vermouth.[17]

BEN REED'S DRY MANHATTAN

Ben Reed, an award-winning bartender with many books to his credit, has been referred to as the "crown prince of cocktails." In The Art of the Cocktail, *he advises that people who like stronger flavors should experiment with bourbon. Reed comments anecdotally on his experience that the Dry Manhattan is the least popular of all of the Manhattans. This seems to be supported by the literature, as few recipes for Dry Manhattans are recorded. In his many books Reed always features recipes for the Manhattan, the Dry Manhattan, and the Perfect Manhattan. Reed uses a lemon peel to differentiate the Dry Manhattan from the Sweet (cherry) and Perfect (orange) Manhattans.[18]*

1½ ounces rye whiskey
¾ ounce dry vermouth
Dash Angostura bitters
Lemon zest, to garnish

Add the ingredients to a mixing glass filled with ice (first ensure that all the ingredients are very cold), and stir the mixture until chilled. Strain into a frosted Martini glass, add the garnish, and serve.

JULEP MANHATTAN

If Dale DeGroff is the "king" of cocktails, and Ben Reed is the "crown prince," then Joy Perrine is a grand duchess. Joy is a longtime bartender at Jack's Lounge in Louisville, Kentucky, and the coauthor of The Kentucky Bourbon Cocktail Book, *which features ten Manhattans, including the classic three Manhattans plus other recipes such as the Darkened Manhattan (coffee based), Peach Manhattan, and Summer Manhattan. Here is her recipe for the Julep Manhattan.*[19]

2 ounces Kentucky bourbon
¼ ounce white crème de menthe
¼ ounce Noilly Prat dry vermouth
3–4 drops Angostura bitters

Combine ingredients, shake over ice, and strain into a chilled Martini glass. Garnish with a sprig of fresh mint.

MANHATTAN SOUTH

The Complete Bartender by Robyn Feller presents more than two thousand recipes for cocktails and features four recipes for the Manhattan: the Manhattan, Manhattan (Dry), Manhattan (Perfect), and Manhattan South. This recipe uses gin instead of whiskey.[20]

1 ounce gin
½ ounce dry vermouth
½ ounce Southern Comfort
Dash Angostura bitters

Fill mixing glass with ice. Add gin, dry vermouth, Southern Comfort, and bitters. Stir. Strain into a chilled cocktail glass.

ST. MORITZ MANHATTAN
(AKA SIDNEY MANHATTAN)

Robert Plotkin is the author of many books, including The Bartender's Companion: The Original Guide to American Cocktails and Drinks. *He includes over sixty recipes for the Manhattan in his book.*[21]

¼ ounce dry vermouth
¼ ounce Green Chartreuse
3 dashes orange bitters
1½ ounces bourbon

Pour ingredients into iced mixing glass. Stir and strain. Garnish with a lemon twist and serve in a chilled cocktail glass.

THE PERFECT MANHATTAN

A Perfect Manhattan has both sweet and dry vermouth. Reed comments in his book *The Art of the Cocktail* that "perfect" refers to the balance between sweet and dry.[22]

BEN REED'S PREMIUM MANHATTAN

This recipe is for a Premium Manhattan, which also happens to be a Perfect Manhattan.

1¾ ounces Knob Creek bourbon
¾ ounce Vya dry vermouth
¾ ounce Vya sweet vermouth
Dash Angostura bitters
Orange zest, to garnish

Add all the ingredients to a mixing glass filled with ice, and stir gently with a bar spoon. Strain into a frosted Martini glass and garnish with orange zest.

THE WHITE MANHATTAN

Brian Downing is a bartender in Louisville, Kentucky, but is originally from northern Virginia and worked as a bartender at Clyde's in the Washington, DC, area. Brian presented this version of a Manhattan at the Southern

Wines and Spirits, Spirits and Service Academy held at Sullivan University in the first part of 2014. Brian uses all white ingredients for a near crystal-clear drink. The sweet Dolin Blanc vermouth is balanced by the dry Cinzano Blanco. Downing suggests garnishing with white cherries to stay with the theme; however, red cherries can be used for good color contrast between the drink and the garnish.

1 ounce New Make rye
½ ounce Dolin Blanc vermouth
¾ ounce Cinzano Blanco vermouth
Dash Regan's #6 orange bitters

In a mixing glass, combine the whiskey, vermouth, and bitters. Add ice and stir. Strain into a chilled cocktail glass. Garnish with the cherry and a twist.

MODERN MANHATTANS

Even though it is very difficult to improve upon a drink like the Manhattan, with a little tweak here or there, you have a completely new drink based on the classic cocktail. The following drinks are riffs on the Manhattan cocktail.

JUST FOR MARY

Tony Abou-Ganim, once an aspiring actor, is the bartender's bartender. Tony has been mixing cocktails for over three decades and has worked on both the East and West coasts. He currently lives in Las Vegas, where he helped to open the Bellagio, serving as its first "mixologist."(In 1998, that title was groundbreaking in the bartending world.) He has invented many cocktails, including the Cable Car. Tony now owns his own company, the Modern Mixologist. This version of a Manhattan was created by Tony for his coauthor, Mary Elizabeth Faulkner, and their book, The Modern Mixologist: Contemporary Classic Cocktails.[23]

2 ounces straight rye whiskey
½ ounce Cherry Heering
½ ounce Lillet Blond
2 dashes Regan's #6 orange bitters

In an ice-filled glass, add the rye whiskey, Cherry Heering, Lillet Blond, and the orange bitters. Stir until very cold. Strain into a chilled cocktail glass. Finish with essence of a burned orange twist (then discard the orange). Garnish with a brandied cherry.

TUESDAY MEZCAL MANHATTAN

Bartender Susie Hoyt is the beverage director at the Silver Dollar and El Camino in Louisville, Kentucky. She is a New York native who grew up in small-town Ohio before moving to Chicago after graduating from Miami University of Ohio with a degree in public relations and political science. Susie presented this version of a Manhattan at the Southern Wines and Spirits, Spirits and Service Academy held at Sullivan University in 2014. She concocted this Manhattan on the spot and walked away with top honors.

1¼ ounces Wild Turkey rye 101
½ ounce Cardinal Mendoza Solera Spanish brandy
½ ounce Dolin Rouge
¼ ounce Punt e Mes
¼ ounce Mezcal
Dash Angostura bitters
Dash Regan's #6 orange bitters

Stir in a mixing glass until correct temperature and dilution is reached and strain into a chilled coupe glass or cocktail glass. Express light lemon oil and orange oil on the bottom of the outside of the glass.

MANHATTAN JELLO SHOT

If you don't want to drink a Manhattan, perhaps you'd like to eat one! Michelle Palm takes the Manhattan to a solid form in her book Jelly Shot Test Kitchen.[24]

⅔ cup bitters syrup
2 envelops Knox gelatin
⅔ cup bourbon
⅔ cup Italian sweet vermouth
Maraschino cherries, diced small for garnish,
    if desired

Pour the bitters syrup (recipe follows) into a medium saucepan and sprinkle with the gelatin. Allow the gelatin to soak for a minute or two. Heat over very low heat until gelatin is dissolved, stirring constantly, about 5 minutes. Remove from heat and stir in the bourbon and the sweet vermouth. Pour into loaf pan and refrigerate until fully set, several hours or overnight. To serve, cut into desired shapes and garnish with the diced maraschino, if desired. Makes 18 to 24 jello shots.

BITTER SYRUP

1½ cups water
1 cup granulated sugar
9 tablespoons Angostura bitters

Combine all ingredients in a medium saucepan. Heat over medium heat until mixture boils, stirring occasionally. Remove from heat and allow to cool to room temperature.

AÑEJO MANHATTAN

In 2010, I attended the International Association of Culinary Professionals (IACP) conference in Portland, Oregon. At the time the IACP had a mentorship program in which experienced authors were matched with new or up-and-coming authors. I was paired with Kara New-man, now the spirits editor of the Wine Enthusiast. *Kara gave me some great advice! She featured a recipe for an Añejo Manhattan in her book* Spice and Ice. *Kara writes that she adapted this recipe from Ryan Magarian, who garnishes the drink "with a tequila soaked dried cherry wrapped in spicy mole salami."[25]*

2 ounces Añejo tequila
½ ounce sweet vermouth
¼ ounce Licor 43
Dash Angostura bitters
Dash Regan's #6 orange bitters

Combine all ingredients in a pint glass. Fill the glass three-quarters full of ice. Stir swiftly for 30 seconds and strain into a cocktail glass.

MADISON AVENUE MANHATTANS
(MANHATTANS FOR A CROWD)

In 2013, I was honored to sit next to Kara Newman at a book signing at the Bourbon Classic in downtown Louisville at the Art Center. She was autographing copies of her new book, Cocktails for a Crowd: More than 40 Recipes for Making Popular Drinks in Party-Pleasing Batches, *and I was signing both* The Old Fashioned *and* The Kentucky Bourbon Cookbook. *The Madison Avenue Manhattan recipe was featured in her new book for people looking to fix drinks for a group of people. Kara credits this drink to a friend named Nora who threw a* Mad Men–*themed party. Kara also features the Bobby Burns cocktail, named for Scottish poet Robert Burns, which is a Scotch version that is very similar to the Manhattan.*[26]

16 ounces (2 cups) rye whiskey
8 ounces (1 cup) sweet vermouth
4 ounces (½ cup) water
1 teaspoon Angostura bitters
8 brandied cherries, for garnish (see recipe below)

In a pitcher that holds at least 4 cups, combine the whiskey, vermouth, water, and bitters and stir well. Using a funnel, decant into a 1-liter liquor bottle or two 750-ml liquor bottles. Cap tightly and refrigerate for at least 2 hours, until chilled. To serve, set out a bowl or wine bucket filled with ice. Shake the bottle to ensure the cocktail is well mixed, then set it in the ice so it stays chilled. Pour into coupe glasses and garnish each drink with a cherry, if desired.

BRANDIED CHERRIES

½ cup sugar

4 ounces (½ cup) water

½ cup dried cherries

¼ teaspoon almond or vanilla extract

4 ounces (½) cup brandy, bourbon, aged rum, or
    other brown spirit, plus more as needed

In a small saucepan, combine the sugar and water over medium-high heat. Cook, stirring constantly, until the sugar is dissolved and the syrup boiling. Lower the heat to maintain a simmer, then stir in the cherries and almond extract. Simmer uncovered, stirring occasionally, until the liquid thickens to a light syrupy consistency, 5 to 7 minutes. Remove from the heat, stir in the brandy, and let cool to room temperature. Transfer the cherries and liquid to a 1-quart glass jar or other glass container with a lid. Add more brandy if needed to cover the cherries. Covered and stored in the refrigerator, the cherries will keep for about 2 weeks.

WALNUT MANHATTAN

The Walnut Manhattan comes from a New York estab-lishment, Schiller's Liquor Bar, for which a four-book compilation was completed by Keith McNally. This recipe is featured in the Classic Cocktails *book, and the Maple Simple Syrup is listed in* The Bartender's Guide.[27]

2½ ounce Alibi American whiskey
½ ounce Antica Formula vermouth
½ ounce maple simple syrup (see recipe below)
5 dashes Fee Brothers black walnut bitters

Pour the whiskey, Antica Formula vermouth, maple simple syrup, and bitters into a mixing glass with ice. Stir well with a bar spoon for 40 to 45 revolutions and strain into a chilled Martini glass.

MAPLE SIMPLE SYRUP

2¼ cups water
1¾ cups pure maple syrup
Dash nutmeg
Dash cinnamon

Place the water, maple syrup, nutmeg, and cinnamon in a medium saucepan. Heat over medium heat until just below boiling, stirring constantly until the consistency is even. Remove from heat and allow the syrup to cool to room temperature. Transfer the syrup to a clean mason jar, seal tightly, and refrigerate. It will keep for a little less than 1 month in the refrigerator.

NUTTY MANHATTAN

The Nutty Manhattan is featured in the book Hip Sips *by Lucy Brennan. Brennan is the owner of Mint and 820 in Portland, Oregon. In this recipe, Brennan uses a walnut liqueur as the modifier in the Manhattan.*[28]

2½ ounces Maker's Mark bourbon
½ ounce Nocello liqueur
1 maraschino cherry
Cocktail ice cubes for chilling and shaking

Fill a 5-ounce Martini glass with ice and set aside to chill. Fill a tempered pint glass with ice; then add the bourbon and Nocello. Cap the glass with a stainless steel cocktail shaker and shake vigorously for 10 seconds. Empty the ice from the Martini glass and strain the drink into the chilled glass. Garnish with the cherry and serve immediately.

SMOKED MANHATTAN

Against the Grain Brewery and Restaurant in Louisville, Kentucky, is located at the River Bats ball field. Against the Grain cold-smokes the rye in this smoked Manhattan.

1½ ounces cold-smoked Templeton rye
¾ ounce sweet vermouth
2 dashes Bourbon Barrel Aged bitters
2 dashes Bourbon Barrel Aged vanilla

Pour ingredients into ice-filled mixing glass and stir vigorously. Strain into a chilled cocktail glass.

METS MANHATTAN

Ray Foley is the publisher of Bartender Magazine *and the author of* Bartender Magazine's Ultimate Bartender's Guide. *In his book he lists over thirteen hundred drinks from "the world's best bartenders." Included is the Mets Manhattan.*[29]

2 ounces Crown Royal
¼ ounce Martini & Rossi dry vermouth
¼ ounce strawberry schnapps

Pour ingredients into ice-filled mixing glass and stir vigorously. Strain into a chilled cocktail glass. A strawberry garnish is optional.

CHAMPAGNE MANHATTAN

This next cocktail was inspired by a note in Kester Thompson's book, Cocktails, Cocktails and More Cocktails, *in which he lists recipes for all three shades of Manhattans in both metric and imperial measurements. He doesn't provide an explicit recipe for the Champagne Manhattan, but what a great idea![30]*

1 ounce bourbon
½ ounce sweet vermouth
1 or 2 dashes bitters
5 ounces champagne
1 orange twist, for garnish

Add the bourbon, vermouth, and bitters to a champagne flute. Add the champagne and allow the mixture to blend; then twist an orange peel over the glass, sink it into the drink, and serve.

THE MALONEY #2

Each year Food and Wine *magazine publishes a book of cocktails. Bartenders and mixologists from around the country, including such mixing stars as Tony Abou-Ganim, Kathy Casey, Adam Seger, and Bridget Albert, contribute their best cocktails. The compilation is edited by Kate Krader, aided by deputy editor and mixology superstar Jim Meehan. Kentucky native bartender Josh Durr contributed several recipes to* Food and Wine Cocktails, 2013, *including the Maloney #2, a riff on a Manhattan. Durr insists on a 100 proof and/or bonded whiskey because "you need the higher proof to balance the cocktail. Lower proofs fall flat on the tongue."* [31]

1½ ounces bonded bourbon, such as Old Fitzgerald
    bottled in bond 100 proof
1½ ounces sweet vermouth
¾ ounce Cynar (bitter artichoke aperitif)
¼ ounce maraschino liqueur
1 orange twist, for garnish

In a mixing glass, combine the bourbon, vermouth, Cynar, and maraschino liqueur; fill with ice and stir well. Strain into a chilled, ice-filled double rocks glass and garnish with the orange twist.

THE OLD HOUSE ROB ROY

The Rob Roy is a Manhattan made with Scotch rather than American whiskey. The Rob Roy is featured in The Old House Holiday and Party Cookbook.[32]

¾ ounce sweet vermouth
1½ ounces Scotch whiskey
Dash orange bitters

Stir well with cracked ice and strain into a cocktail glass.

THE BULL AND BEAR BRONX COCKTAIL

The Bull and Bear Bar is located on the ground floor of the Waldorf Astoria in New York City. Many great cocktails were created at this bar, including the Bronx, the Bobbie Burns, and the Rob Roy.[33]

3 ounces gin
1½ ounces fresh orange juice
Dash of French dry vermouth
Dash of Italian sweet vermouth
1 orange twist

In an ice-filled cocktail shaker, combine all liquid ingredients. Cover and shake thoroughly.

Strain into a chilled cocktail glass. Garnish with an orange twist.

SPANISH MANHATTAN

This first modern Manhattan hails from the New York restaurant Suba, which closed in 2009. This version of the Manhattan employs sweet sherry instead of sweet vermouth.[34]

2 ounces Maker's Mark bourbon
1 ounce Lustau sherry
2 dashes Peychaud's bitters

In an ice-filled cocktail shaker, combine the bourbon, sherry, and bitters. Stir and strain into a chilled cocktail glass.

MANHATTAN'S BIG APPLE

This recipe is inspired by a combination of the concoctions of master mixologist Ben Reed and Robert Plotkin, who both list an apple-based Manhattan in their books: Reed an Apple Manhattan made with Calvados, and Plotkin an Apple Manhattan with Beretzen apple liqueur.[35]

2 ounces applejack brandy
½ ounce sweet vermouth
½ ounce dry vermouth
2 dashes Bar Keep baked apple bitters
Granny Smith apple wedge, to garnish

Add all the ingredients to a mixing glass filled with ice and stir gently with a bar spoon. Strain into a frosted Martini glass and garnish with an apple wedge.

DALE DEGROFF'S
MILLIONAIRE'S MANHATTAN

Dale DeGroff, King Cocktail, gives three modern "Manhattan" cocktails in his book The Essential Cocktail: The Art of Mixing Perfect Drinks, *even though he concedes that cocktail traditionalists and Manhattan purists might not view the Millionaire's Manhattan as an authentic Manhattan.*[36]

Orange slice
Edible gold flakes
1½ ounces Woodford Reserve bourbon
½ ounce Grand Marnier Centenaire
1 ounce unsweetened pineapple juice
¼ ounce orgeat

Frost the rim of the glass using the orange slice and the gold leaf, and set in the freezer to chill. DeGroff suggests setting up frosted glasses several hours before serving. Shake the bourbon, Grand Marnier, pineapple juice, and orgeat in a mixing glass with ice. Strain into the prepared glass with no garnish other than the extravagantly decorated rim.

SCOTT BEATTIE'S
FRANKFORT MANHATTAN

Scott Beattie is a mixologist and the author of Artisanal Cocktails. *His book presents cocktails according to the four seasons. Beattie identifies the Manhattan as a "spring" cocktail, but writes that the drink is served year-round at Cyrus Restaurant in Healdsburg, California. One of the interesting features of this version of the Manhattan is Beattie's infused bourbon (see recipe below). Beattie reports that demand for the infused bourbon is such that it requires the staff at Cyrus to produce the special bourbon by the case. During production the bourbon must be held in a container large enough to catch the oil spray of the citrus zest. According to Beattie, this bourbon is good to mix in drinks or to sip by itself.*[37]

2¼ ounces bourbon infused with vanilla and
     citrus peel
¾ ounce Noilly Prat sweet vermouth
3 dashes Angostura bitters
2 Amarena cherries, for garnish

Place a cocktail glass in the freezer to chill. Combine the bourbon, sweet vermouth, and bitters in a mixing glass and stir well. Add enough ice to fill the mixing glass three-quarters full and stir for 15 seconds more. Strain into the chilled glass and garnish with two Amarena cherries skewered on a pick.

BOURBON INFUSED WITH VANILLA AND CITRUS PEEL

1 (1-liter) bottle W. L. Weller 12-year-old bourbon
or other well-aged bourbon
1 orange, unwaxed and scrubbed
1 lemon, unwaxed and scrubbed
1 vanilla bean

Pour the bourbon into a large airtight container. Using a ¼-inch-wide zester, zest the orange and lemon over and into the container. Avoid the bitter white pith as much as possible and try to make long, shoestring-like zests. Split the vanilla bean pod lengthwise and turn it inside out. Don't remove the seeds. Add the vanilla pod to the bourbon. Close the container and store it in a dark, cool place. Stir the bourbon mixture once per day for a week to mix the ingredients. After 1 week, carefully pour the infused bourbon back into the bottle. Add 1 strip each of the orange and lemon zests and the vanilla bean, then seal up the bottle.

WOODFORD RESERVE MANHATTANS

The Brown-Forman Corporation in Louisville, Kentucky, holds an annual contest for bartenders in the creation of new twists on the Manhattan. The winner earns the title Master of the Manhattan. Below are some of the recipes featured on the Woodford Reserve's website for Manhattans.

FRENCH MANHATTAN

2 ounces Woodford Reserve bourbon
1 ounce Chambord liqueur
Dash of bitters

Shake ingredients with ice and strain into a Martini glass. Garnish with a lemon twist.

T-TIME MANHATTAN

2½ ounces Woodford Reserve bourbon
1 ounce Tuaca liqueur
2 dashes blood orange bitters
Dash nutmeg

Shake ingredients with ice and strain into a cocktail glass. Garnish with an orange twist and a cherry.

CITRUS MANHATTAN

1½ ounces Woodford Reserve bourbon
¾ ounce simple syrup
¾ ounce fresh lemon juice
½ ounce fresh orange juice
1 pinch ground cloves
Dash Angostura bitters

Shake ingredients with ice and strain into a cocktail glass. Garnish with a twist of orange.

AND FINALLY . . .

Now it's your turn to create your own Manhattan cocktail. First, pick your favorite spirit, then choose your favorite modifier (or two) and the bitters of your choice. Have fun, and make yours a tasty creation!

YOUR OWN MANHATTAN COCKTAIL

_____ ounces _____(name your spirit)

_____ ounces _____(name your modifier)

_____ ounces _____(if you have
another modifier)

_____ dashes _____bitters

Other ingredients:_____

_____

_____

Your directions:_____

_____

_____

_____

_____

_____

_____

Acknowledgments

Many people contributed to the completion of this book. First and foremost, I would like to thank my wife, Kimberly, for her advice; my sons, Thomas and Michael; my parents, Thomas and Elizabeth Schmid; and my "Kentucky parents," Richard Dunn and the late Carol Dunn: I truly appreciate the love and support of all my family.

Thanks are also due to the following people for their direct or indirect support of this project:

My brother and sisters and their spouses, Gretchen, Tiffany, Rachel, Justin, Bennett, Ana, Shane, and John: I always enjoy drinking a Manhattan with you!

Thomas J. Smith and Tammy Logston, for making me look good.

Bill Noel, friend and mentor, thank you for your ideas and, most of all, for sharing your experience.

Adam Seger, friend, thank you for your advice, your energy, and for constantly raising the bar.

Gary Gruver, for your mentorship related to bartending.

John Peter LaLoganes, my friend, thank you for your advice and support.

Scot Duval, for your friendship and friendly counsel.

Ashley Runyon, for believing in me.

Quinten and Tresa Moser, friends, thank you for your support.

Brian and Angie Clute, friends and fellow cocktail lovers.

Joy Perrine, bartender extraordinaire, for your business savvy and your energy.

My brothers and sisters in the United States Bartenders' Guild, thank you for your support, guidance, and mentorship.

Chancellor A. R. Sullivan, for leading the university at which I work and for your support.

President of Sullivan University Glenn Sullivan, for your love of the Bluegrass State's beverage, bourbon, and for your advice and support.

Dr. Jay Marr, for your support and advice.

Dr. Ken Miller, for your advice and for believing in me.

Dr. Stephen Coppock, friend and mentor, thank you for always seeing the light side of everything and for your jokes.

David H. Dodd, MBE, thank you for leading by example, and for your perspective and your wisdom.

Allen Akmon, John Foster, Kimberly Jones, Derek Spendlove, Rob Beighey, the directors and chairs of the programs at Sullivan University's National Center for Hospitality Studies, thank you for your leadership and example.

Finally, I would like to thank the following musical artists, whose music I listened to when writing this book: Justin Timberlake, Keb' Mo', Albert Cummings, B. B. King, Buddy Guy, Darius Rucker, Robert Cray, Dave Matthews, David Holmes, Dr. Dre, Etta James, Jay-Z, Kid Rock, Johnny Cash, Keith Sweat, Pharrell Williams, Alicia Keys, and Sheryl Crow.

Notes

1. THE MANHATTAN COCKTAIL

1. Robert Plotkin, *Secrets Revealed of America's Greatest Cocktails: The Hottest Spirits, Coolest Drinks, and Freshest Places* (Tucson, AZ: Bar Media, 2007), 59; Michael Jackson, *Bar and Cocktail Companion* (Philadelphia: Running Press, 1994), 192.

2. David Embury, *The Fine Art of Mixing Drinks* (New York: Mud Puddle Books, 2009), 121; David Wondrich, *Esquire Drinks: An Opinionated and Irreverent Guide to Drinking* (New York: Hearst Books, 2002), 54; Kingsley Amis, *Everyday Drinking* (New York: Bloomsbury USA, 2008), 23; Irvin S. Cobb, *Irvin S. Cobb's Own Recipe Book* (Louisville: Frankfort Distilleries, 1934), 41; Gary Regan, *The Joy of Mixology* (New York: Clarkson Potter, 2003), 285; Robert Hess, *The Essential Bartender's Pocket Guide* (New York: Mud Puddle Books, 2009), 79.

3. Eben Klemm, *The Cocktail Primer* (Kansas City: Andrew McMeel, 2009), 41; Embury, *The Fine Art of Mixing Drinks*, 115; Joseph Scott and Donald Bain, *The World's Best Bartender's Guide* (New York: HP Books, 1998), 109.

4. Dale DeGroff, *The Craft of the Cocktail* (New York: Clarkson Potter, 2002), 138; David Wondrich, *Imbibe!* (New York: Perigee, 2007), 237–38.

5. Paul Harrington and Laura Moorhead, *Cocktail: The Drinks Bible for the 21st Century* (New York: Viking-Penguin, 1998), 114; Wondrich, *Imbibe!* 238; Brian Murphy, *See, Mix, Drink: A Refreshingly Simple Guide to Crafting the World's Most Popular Cocktails* (New York: Little, Brown, 2011), 62–63, 196–97.

6. Regan, *The Joy of Mixology*, 286; Wondrich, *Imbibe!* 238; Harrington and Moorhead, *Cocktail*, 114. The suggested connection between the Manhattan cocktail and the Manhattan Club in the late 1800s might have inspired other cocktail/club associations, such as the Old Fashioned Whiskey cocktail with the Pendennis Club. Albert W. A. Schmid, *The Old Fashioned Whiskey Cocktail* (Lexington: University Press of Kentucky, 2013).

7. Mittie Hellmich, *Mini-bar Whiskey: A Little Book of Big Drinks* (San Francisco: Chronicle, 2008), 29.

8. Regan, *The Joy of Mixology*, 285; Plotkin, *Secrets Revealed of America's Greatest Cocktails*, 59; Tom Stevenson, *The Sotheby's Wine Encyclopedia*, 4th ed. (London: Dorling Kindersley, 2007), 31; Karen MacNeil, *The Wine Bible* (New York: Workman, 2001), 334; Jancis Robinson, *The Oxford Companion to Wine*, 2nd ed. (Oxford: Oxford University Press, 1999), 739; Jared Brown and Anistatia Miller, *The Mixellany: Guide to Vermouth and Other Aperitifs* (Upper Slaughter, UK: Mixellany, 2011), 68–131.

9. Stephanie Rosenbaum, *The Art of Vintage Cocktails* (Philadelphia: Egg & Dart, 2011), 32; Wondrich, *Imbibe!* 237; Plotkin, *Secrets Revealed of America's Greatest Cocktails*, 59.

10. Hess, *The Essential Bartender's Pocket Guide*, 79; Plotkin, *Secrets Revealed of America's Greatest Cocktails*, 59; Stevenson, *The Sotheby's Wine Encyclopedia*, 31; Vincent Gasnier, *Drinks* (London: Dorling Kindersley, 2007), 150; Rosenbaum, *The Art of Vintage Cocktails*, 32; Ben Reed, *The Art of the Cocktail* (London: Ryland, Peters & Small, 2009), 89.

11. Embury, *The Fine Art of Mixing Drinks*, 123.

12. Brad Thomas Parsons, *Bitters: A Spirited History of a Classic Cure-all with Cocktails, Recipes and Formulas* (Berkeley: Ten Speed, 2011), 9, 108; Molly Wellman, *Handcrafted Cocktails: The Mixologist's Guide to Classic Drinks for Morning, Noon and Night* (Cincinnati: Betterway Home, 2013), 37; Jackson, *Bar and Cocktail Companion*, 192; Regan, *The Joy of Mixology*, 287.

13. Dale DeGroff, *The Essential Cocktail: The Art of Mixing Perfect Drinks* (New York: Clarkson Potter, 2008), 34; Wondrich, *Esquire Drinks*, 54; Anthony Giglio, *Cocktails in New York: Where to Find 100 Classics and How to Make Them at Home* (New York: Rizzoli International, 2004), 46; Regan, *The Joy of Mixology*, 287.

14. Plotkin, *Secrets Revealed of America's Greatest Cocktails*, 68–79; Embury, *The Fine Art of Mixing Drinks*, 123.

15. Embury, *The Fine Art of Mixing Drinks*, 123.

16. Hess, *The Essential Bartender's Pocket Guide*, 79; Rosenbaum, *The Art of Vintage Cocktails*, 32; Tony Abou-Ganim and Mary Elizabeth Faulkner, *The Modern Mixologist: Contemporary Classic Cocktails* (Chicago: Surrey Books, 2010), 47; Jason Kosmas and Dushan Zaric, *Speakeasy: Classic Cocktails Reimagined, from New York's Employees Only Bar* (Berkeley: Ten Speed, 2010), 34–36.

17. Albert Stevens Crockett, *The Old Waldorf-Astoria Bar Book* (New York: A. S. Crockett, 1935); Embury, *The Fine Art of Mixing Drinks*, 122.

2. PLACES, PEOPLE, AND MANHATTAN COCKTAIL LORE

1. Ben Reed, *Cool Cocktails: The Hottest New Drinks and the Best of the Classics* (London: Ryland, Peters & Small, 2000), 60.

2. Plotkin, *Secrets Revealed of America's Greatest Cocktails*, 59.

3. RECIPES

1. Pete Wells, "Frost on the Sun: Summertime Cocktails," *New York Times*, June 21, 2006; Jerry Thomas, *Jerry Thomas' Bar-tenders Guide* (New York: Dick & Fitzgerald, 1887), 24.

2. DeGroff, *The Essential Cocktail*, 34.

3. Kosmas and Zaric, *Speakeasy*, 34; Keith McNally, *Schiller's Liquor Bar: Classic Cocktails* (New York: Clarkson Potter, 2013), 30–31.

4. New York Bartenders' Association, *Official Handbook and Guide* (New York: New York Bartenders' Association, 1895), 32–33.

5. Tim Daly, *Daly's Bartenders' Encyclopedia* (Worchester, MA.: Tim Daly, 1903), 8, 59.

6. Daly, *Daly's Bartenders' Encyclopedia*, 49.

7. Cobb, *Irvin S. Cobb's Own Recipe Book*, 41.

8. John E. Kleber, ed., *The Encyclopedia of Louisville* (Lexington: University Press of Kentucky, 2001), 674.

9. *The Bacardi Party Book* (Miami: Bacardi Imports, 1972), 5.

10. Amis, *Everyday Drinking*, 23–24.

11. DeGroff, *The Craft of the Cocktail*, 138; DeGroff, *The Essential Cocktail*, 34. The quote from Bourdain is taken from the back cover of *The Essential Cocktail*.

12. David Renton, *David Renton's Dorchester Cocktail Book* (London: George Weidenfeld & Nicolson, 1988), 27, 30.

13. Kit Wohl, *Arnaud's Restaurant Cookbook: New Orleans Legendary Creole Cuisine* (Gretna, LA: Pelican, 2005), 171–75.

14. Giglio, *Cocktails in New York*, 25.

15. Lara Nixon, *A Is for Absinthe: A Spirited Book of ABC's* (self-published, 2014).

16. Murphy, *See, Mix, Drink*, 30–31, 196–97.

17. Renton, *David Renton's Dorchester Cocktail Book*, 30.

18. Reed, *The Art of the Cocktail*, 89.

19. Joy Perrine and Susan Reigler, *The Kentucky Bourbon Cocktail Book* (Lexington: University Press of Kentucky, 2009), 51.

20. Robyn M. Feller, *The Complete Bartender* (New York: Berkley Books, 1990), 290–91.

21. Robert Plotkin, *The Bartender's Companion: The Original Guide to American Cocktails and Drinks*, 5th ed. (Tucson, AZ: Bar Media, 2004), 152.

22. Renton, *David Renton's Dorchester Cocktail Book*, 30; Reed, *The Art of the Cocktail*, 89.

23. Abou-Ganim and Faulkner, *The Modern Mixologist*, 137.

24. Michelle Palm, *Jelly Shot Test Kitchen: Jelling Classic Cocktails—One Drink at a Time* (Philadelphia: Running Press, 2011), 127.

25. Kara Newman, *Spice and Ice: 60 Tongue-Tingling Cocktails* (San Francisco: Chronicle, 2009), 144.

26. Kara Newman, *Cocktails for a Crowd: More than 40 Recipes for Making Popular Drinks in Party-Pleasing Batches* (San Francisco: Chronicle, 2013), 23, 79; Schmid, *The Old Fashioned Whiskey Cocktail;* Albert W. A. Schmid, *The Kentucky Bourbon Cookbook* (Lexington: University Press of Kentucky, 2010).

27. McNally, *Schiller's Liquor Bar: Classic Cocktails*, 87; Keith McNally, *Schiller's Liquor Bar: The Bartender's Guide* (New York: Clarkson Potter, 2013), 60, 63.

28. Lucy Brennan, *Hip Sips* (San Francisco: Chronicle, 2006), 75.

29. Ray Foley, *Bartender Magazine's Ultimate Bartender's Guide* (Naperville, IL: Sourcebooks, 2007), 70.

30. Kester Thompson, *Cocktails, Cocktails and More Cocktails* (Watertown, MA: Imagine, 2011), 107.

31. Kate Krader and Jim Meehan, eds., *Food and Wine Cocktails, 2013* (New York: American Express, 2013), 116.

32. Erma Biesel Dick, *The Old House Holiday and Party Cookbook* (New York: Cowles, 1969), 209.

33. Giglio, *Cocktails in New York*, 38.

34. Ibid., 46.

35. Reed, *The Art of the Cocktail*, 91; Plotkin, *The Bartender's Companion*, 147.

36. DeGroff, *The Essential Cocktail*, 242.

37. Scott Beattie, *Artisanal Cocktails* (Berkeley: Ten Speed, 2008), 65, 72.

Bibliography

Abou-Ganim, Tony, and Mary Elizabeth Faulkner. *The Modern Mixologist: Contemporary Classic Cocktails*. Chicago: Surrey Books, 2010.

Amis, Kingsley. *Everyday Drinking*. New York: Bloomsbury USA, 2008.

The Bacardi Party Book. Miami: Bacardi Imports, 1972.

Beattie, Scott. *Artisanal Cocktails*. Berkeley: Ten Speed, 2008.

Berk, Sally Ann, ed. *The New York Bartender's Guide*. New York: Black Dog & Leventhal, 2005.

Brennan, Lucy. *Hip Sips*. San Francisco: Chronicle, 2006.

Brown, Jared, and Anistatia Miller. *The Mixellany: Guide to Vermouth and Other Aperitifs*. Upper Slaughter, UK: Mixellany, 2011.

Bykofsky, Sheree, and Megan Buckley. *Sexy City Cocktails: Stylish Drinks and Cool Classics You Can Sip with Attitude*. Avon, MA: Adams Media, 2003.

Cobb, Irvin S. *Irvin S. Cobb's Own Recipe Book*. Louisville: Frankfort Distilleries, 1934.

Cotton, Leo, ed. *Old Mr. Boston de Luxe Official Bartender's Guide*. 1935. Reprint, Boston: Mr. Boston Distiller Corporation, 1972.

Crockett, Albert Stevens. *The Old Waldorf-Astoria Bar Book*. New York: A. S. Crockett, 1935.

Daly, Tim. *Daly's Bartenders' Encyclopedia*. Worcester, MA: Tim Daly, 1903.

DeGroff, Dale. *The Craft of the Cocktail*. New York: Clarkson Potter, 2002.

———. *The Essential Cocktail: The Art of Mixing Perfect Drinks*. New York: Clarkson Potter, 2008.

Dick, Erma Biesel. *The Old House Holiday and Party Cookbook*. New York: Cowles, 1969.

Embury, David A. *The Fine Art of Mixing Drinks*. New York: Mud Puddle Books, 1948, 1952, 1958, 1980, 1986, 2008, 2009.

Feller, Robyn M. *The Complete Bartender*. New York: Berkley Books, 1990.

Foley, Ray, ed. *The Bar Guide: William-Sonoma*. San Francisco: Weldon Owen, 2006.

———. *Bartender Magazine's Ultimate Bartender's Guide*. Naperville, IL: Sourcebooks, 2007.

Gasnier, Vincent. *Drinks*. London: Dorling Kindersley, 2007.

Giglio, Anthony. *Cocktails in New York: Where to Find 100 Classics and How to Make Them at Home*. New York: Rizzoli International, 2004.

Harrington, Paul, and Laura Moorhead. *Cocktail: The Drinks Bible for the 21st Century*. New York: Viking-Penguin, 1998.

Hess, Robert. *The Essential Bartender's Pocket Guide*. New York: Mud Puddle Books, 2009.

Jackson, Michael. *Bar and Cocktail Companion*. Philadelphia: Running Press, 1979, 1984, 1994.

Kleber, John E., ed. *The Encyclopedia of Louisville.* Lexington: University Press of Kentucky, 2001.

Klemm, Eben. *The Cocktail Primer.* Kansas City: Andrew McMeel, 2009.

Kosmas, Jason, and Dushan Zaric. *Speakeasy: Classic Cocktails Reimagined, from New York's Employees Only Bar.* Berkeley: Ten Speed, 2010.

Krader, Kate, and Jim Meehan, eds. *Food and Wine Cocktails, 2013.* New York: American Express, 2013.

MacNeil, Karen. *The Wine Bible.* New York: Workman, 2001.

McNally, Keith. *Schiller's Liquor Bar: Classic Cocktails.* New York: Clarkson Potter, 2013.

———. *Schiller's Liquor Bar: The Bartender's Guide* (New York: Clarkson Potter, 2013.

Murphy, Brian. *See, Mix, Drink: A Refreshingly Simple Guide to Crafting the World's Most Popular Cocktails.* New York: Little Brown, 2011.

Newman, Kara. *Cocktails for a Crowd: More than 40 Recipes for Making Popular Drinks in Party-Pleasing Batches.* San Francisco: Chronicle, 2013.

———. *Spice and Ice: 60 Tongue-Tingling Cocktails.* San Francisco: Chronicle, 2009.

New York Bartenders' Association. *Official Handbook and Guide.* New York: New York Bartenders' Association, 1895.

Palm, Michelle. *Jelly Shot Test Kitchen: Jelling Classic Cocktails— One Drink at a Time.* Philadelphia: Running Press, 2011.

Parsons, Brad Thomas. *Bitters: A Spirited History of a Classic Cure-all with Cocktails, Recipes and Formulas.* Berkeley: Ten Speed, 2011.

Perrine, Joy, and Susan Reigler. *The Kentucky Bourbon Cocktail Book.* Lexington: University Press of Kentucky, 2009.

Plotkin, Robert. *The Bartender's Companion: The Original Guide to American Cocktails and Drinks*. 5th ed. Tucson, AZ: Bar Media, 2004.

————. *Secrets Revealed of America's Greatest Cocktails: The Hottest Spirits, Coolest Drinks, and Freshest Places*. Tucson, AZ: Bar Media, 2007.

Reed, Ben. *The Art of the Cocktail*. London: Ryland, Peters & Small, 2004, 2009.

————. *Cool Cocktails: The Hottest New Drinks and the Best of the Classics*. London: Ryland, Peters & Small, 2000.

Regan, Gary. *The Joy of Mixology*. New York: Clarkson Potter, 2003.

Regan, Gary, and Mardee Haidin Regan. *New Classic Cocktails*. New York: Macmillan, 1997.

Renton, David. *David Renton's Dorchester Cocktail Book*. London: George Weidenfeld & Nicolson, 1988.

Robinson, Jancis. *The Oxford Companion to Wine*. 2nd ed. Oxford: Oxford University Press, 1999.

Rosenbaum, Stephanie. *The Art of Vintage Cocktails*. Philadelphia: Egg & Dart, 2011.

Schmid, Albert W. A. *The Kentucky Bourbon Cookbook*. Lexington: University Press of Kentucky, 2010.

————. *The Old Fashioned Whiskey Cocktail*. Lexington: University Press of Kentucky, 2013.

Scott, Joseph, and Donald Bain. *The World's Best Bartender's Guide*. New York: HP Books, 1998.

Stevenson, Tom. *The Sotheby's Wine Encyclopedia*. 4th ed. London: Dorling Kindersley, 2007.

Thomas, Jerry. *Jerry Thomas' Bar-tenders Guide*. New York: Dick & Fitzgerald, 1887.

Thompson, Kester. *Cocktails, Cocktails and More Cocktails*. Watertown, MA: Imagine, 2011.

Wellman, Molly. *Handcrafted Cocktails: The Mixologist's Guide to Classic Drinks for Morning, Noon and Night*. Cincinnati: Betterway Home, 2013.

Wells, Pete. "Frost on the Sun: Summertime Cocktails." *New York Times*, June 21, 2006.

Wohl, Kit. *Arnaud's Restaurant Cookbook: New Orleans Legendary Creole Cuisine*. Gretna, LA: Pelican, 2005.

Wondrich, David. *Esquire Drinks: An Opinionated and Irreverent Guide to Drinking*. New York: Hearst Books, 2002.

———. *Imbibe!* New York: Perigee, 2007.

Index